A souvenir guide

Gawthorpe Hall
Lancashire

National Trust

'Grey, Stately and Picturesque'

When the novelist Charlotte Brontë visited Gawthorpe in 1850, the romantic Elizabethan house was very much to her taste: 'grey, stately and picturesque', she described it, 'a model of old English architecture'. Its Victorian owners, stirred by similar Gothic Revival feelings, were about to transform the house into the ultimate 'old English' home.

Key people

The Rev. Lawrence Shuttleworth (1545–1608), who built the house

Sir James Kay-Shuttleworth (1804–77), who restored and improved the house

Rachel Kay-Shuttleworth (1886–1967), who created the textiles collection

An Elizabethan mansion

The foundation stone of the Hall was laid on 26 August 1600 by the Rev. Lawrence Shuttleworth, whose family had lived at Gawthorpe for over 200 years. Although there is no record of an architect, the design of the building which took shape between 1600 and 1605 – with its three-storey bay windows and ingeniously compact interior – is attributed to Robert Smythson, one of the most influential figures of late Elizabethan architecture.

The Hall was occupied between 1608 and 1669 by Lawrence Shuttleworth's nephew, Colonel Richard Shuttleworth, who fought for Parliament in the Civil War; after his death the family lived elsewhere until 1816, when Robert Shuttleworth, a lawyer, reoccupied the house and began some Neo-classical alterations. Robert, however, died within two years, leaving the property to his infant daughter, Janet, who later married the great Victorian educationalist, Dr James Phillips Kay.

Enhancement as a Victorian home

In the years 1850–52, following his retirement from public service with a baronetcy, Sir James Kay-Shuttleworth employed the architect Sir Charles Barry to restore and improve the Hall in a sympathetic Elizabethan style. Barry heightened the staircase tower, adding openwork parapets, and extensively restored the interior, introducing some rich furnishing schemes in collaboration with A.W.N. Pugin and J.G. Crace. He also laid out a formal garden of Elizabethan design.

A treasury of textiles

Sir James's eldest son, Ughtred (named after a 14th-century ancestor), inherited the estate in 1872, and in 1902 was created Baron Shuttleworth of Gawthorpe. The 4th Lord Shuttleworth moved to the north of Lancashire in 1953, and in 1970 gave the house and grounds to the National Trust, with a long-term lease to Lancashire County Council, for public opening and educational use. This fulfilled the vision of his aunt, the Hon. Rachel Kay-Shuttleworth (1886–1967), whose extensive collections of embroidery, lace and costume were to form the basis of a 'craft house', for the study of textile crafts.

The principal rooms are now restored to their former richness, recreating the sumptuous decorative schemes of Barry, Pugin and Crace. Much of the original furniture is returned on loan from the present Lord Shuttleworth, and a fine collection of 17th-century portraits has been lent by the National Portrait Gallery to represent the family portraits which once populated the Hall, which is now open for you to enjoy.

Gawthorpe Hall from the south-west. Built in 1600–5, its dramatic Elizabethan design is attributed to Robert Smythson. The openwork parapets and tall chimneys were added in 1851 by the Victorian architect Sir Charles Barry.

Tour of the House

The Exterior

The high and compact entrance front of Gawthorpe Hall, with its dramatic succession of three-decker bays presenting a uniform grid of stone mullioned windows, would have been unprecedented in Lancashire when it was built in the early 1600s. Architect Robert Smythson brought with him from his earlier commissions, such as Hardwick Hall in Derbyshire, a very distinctive Elizabethan style. It appears he supplied designs for the two symmetrical elevations seen from the approach – the south-facing entrance front and the west side – allowing local traditions of building to influence the remainder.

The tower and parapets

The staircase tower, engagingly off-centre from every side, has pinnacles of chimneystacks characteristic of Smythson's flamboyant, castle-like style. However, the present chimneys at the four corners of the tower are a Victorian rearrangement by the architect Charles Barry, who raised the tower by one storey and added an openwork parapet. This proudly incorporates the Shuttleworth coat of arms and motto 'Prudentia et Justitia' (Prudence and Justice) on the north and south fronts, while the east and west sides of the tower display the arms and strangely archaic motto of the Kay family, 'Kynd Kynn Knowne Kepe' (Kind Kin Know and Keep). The outer walls are crowned by a parapet of the same Elizabethan openwork pattern, punctuated by corner chimneys and finials, while at ground level a similar balustrade completes Barry's intended framing effect.

The rear elevations

The east and north sides of the building are boldly recessed, echoing Smythson's great rectangular projections at Hardwick but without symmetry. The one ornament of note on the east side is a well-proportioned oriel window with stepped corbelling, a feature which the builders copied from Smythson's grander west front to make the two ends of the Long Gallery look the same. The Padiham sandstone used throughout is laid in courses of varying height, with bands of larger stones above smaller ones. This type of stonework is common in the Pennine region and may relate to the practice of laying the heaviest stones first at each level of scaffolding.

The porch

The front porch was heightened in 1851 to provide a window over the doorway and given a four-centred arch to take a new oak studded external door, where Smythson's porch had had a round-headed archway and internal door. Roman Doric columns and entablature were retained but on higher plinths, while a carved stone plaque of 1605 bearing the Shuttleworth arms of three weaver's shuttles was rescued from the old porch and re-sited above, with the arms of Kay and Kay-Shuttleworth mounted on either side. Decorative ironwork for the front door was designed by Pugin, whose drawings survive for the wicket plate, with its openwork 'KS' monogram, the handle, suspended from weaver's shuttles, and for various other pieces, all of which were made in 1851 by Hardman's of Birmingham.

Left The 'KS' wicket plate designed by Pugin for the front door. It allowed the footman to survey visitors through a small hatch before letting them in

The Entrance Hall

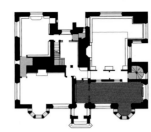

The lofty Entrance Hall, with its openwork wooden screen and tile-floored vestibule, is entirely Charles Barry's creation. Until 1850, the space was occupied by several small rooms on two floors, including a mezzanine bedroom over a low-ceilinged pantry and buttery. The most distinctive feature of Barry's design was the oak screen, panelled and arcaded in an Elizabethan manner. It was constructed in 1851 by William Horne, a Padiham joiner. Oak panelling was continued around the room, framing two internal windows giving light to the adjoining passage. Between these windows was placed a Jacobean panel inlaid with the initials of Shuttleworth ancestors (see p.38), which had formerly been mounted over the fireplace in the demolished mezzanine bedroom.

In the 1850s, the Entrance Hall would have had the formal atmosphere of an ante-room where guests might congregate before dinner. An Edwardian photograph shows it as a billiard room, with a half-size billiard table, some wicker chairs and a set of bobbin-turned chairs upholstered in stamped velvet.

When the 4th Lord Shuttleworth returned to Gawthorpe in 1945 after losing a leg in the war, he turned the room into a ground-floor kitchen, more accessible than the old kitchen in the basement. All the woodwork was dismantled and the archway walled up with asbestos boards clad with panelling on the vestibule side.

Gothic stonework

The magnificently carved stone panel featuring the arms of Sir James Kay-Shuttleworth provides a centrepiece for the arcaded wall in the vestibule. It was made in 1851 as an overmantel for the Entrance Hall fireplace which was originally destined to occupy a cross-wall immediately after the bay. However, in a change of plan, the room was extended fully to the east end, and the fireplace was positioned instead under a window – a favourite device of Barry. The fireplace is robustly castellated in late Gothic style with carved detail to match the great stone archways around the Entrance Hall and vestibule. Its small iron fire grate was dramatically enhanced in 1856 with a Pugin-style surround in coloured marbles incorporating the initials of Sir James's five children.

Only the fireplace and Barry's geometrical ceiling remained intact. However, in 1986 the asbestos wall was demolished and the screen reconstructed. Much of its woodwork had survived in outhouses, and various missing details were re-carved, using the original drawings. A section of panelling was then re-installed to demonstrate the 1850s scheme.

Furniture

Earliest of the old oak pieces is a long sword-chest of *c*.1500, bound with foliated iron straps. The late 17th-century panel-back chair is a fine example of Lancashire carving, with typical motifs of paired sea monsters and a vase of flowers on a mound. A settle of the same date has similar local motifs.

Pictures

The portraits are mid-17th-century. Among those above the panelling is a group of four commemorating Civil War parliamentarians who were imprisoned in Windsor Castle (the tower in the background of each portrait), and who subsequently became royalists. These pictures are on loan from the National Portrait Gallery, as are the two to the left of the fireplace, portraying James Stanley, 7th Earl of Derby, royalist adversary of Col. Richard Shuttleworth, and the redoubtable Charlotte de la Trémoïlle, Countess of Derby, painted as a widow. The remaining portraits, all of which are lent by Lord Kenyon, are of Lancashire contemporaries who figured prominently on the side of either Derby or Shuttleworth.

Textiles

The figured chenille of the curtains is by Alexander Morton & Co., *c*.1920, in a peacock design by Sydney Mawson (1849–1941).

Above The Gothic fireplace in the Entrance Hall

Left Charles Barry's screen in the Entrance Hall

Below One of a set of twelve Sheriff's javelins embossed with the Shuttleworth hand-and-shuttle crest, made in 1864, when Sir James was High Sheriff of Lancashire

If you would like to find out more about the contents of Gawthorpe, see www.nationaltrustcollections.org.uk

The Dining Room

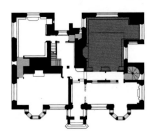

Above
The Dining Room

In the early 17th century this was the great hall, used on grand occasions for dining and for the performance of plays, music and dancing. From 1816 it was more specifically the family Dining Room and was refurnished as such after the room had been restored by Charles Barry in 1851–2. Distinguished guests have included King George V and Queen Mary, who visited in 1913.

The screen
The galleried entrance screen was completed in 1605. The date is inlaid over the two doorways, with the initials of family members and their titles – Hugh Shuttleworth, gentleman, and his three sons, Richard Shuttleworth, knight, Lawrence Shuttleworth, presbyter, and Thomas Shuttleworth, gentleman. The doorways are high enough to have been used as entrances for actors performing plays on a low trestle stage, which the projecting wings of the minstrels' gallery would have overhung.

Restoration in the 1850s

By 1850, the gallery had become unsafe and had to be shored up with pillars, to which Barry added sideboards (grandiosely termed 'beaufettes' on the plan, rather than 'buffets') fitted with shelves and angle mirrors for displaying china. An 18th-century mirror was brought out of the Drawing Room and cut up to provide the mirror panels.

Barry's carved stone chimneypiece of 1851 is superimposed on a much wider 17th-century fireplace with an elliptical arch, the sides of which he concealed with oak panelling and wall benches matching the original woodwork around the rest of the room. The elaborate overmantel displays the coat of arms of Sir James Kay-Shuttleworth flanked by the various shields of (left) Shuttleworth and Kay, and (right) four heiresses who married into the Shuttleworth family – Fleetwood Barton, Jane Kirke, Catherine Clerke and Mary Holden.

The massive cast-iron fire grate and andirons were made in 1852, presumably to Barry's design; but the surrounding encaustic tiles are of c.1880, and may have replaced some 1850s tiles with less robust glazing, notorious for being easily damaged by heat in fireplaces at the Palace of Westminster and elsewhere during that period.

Plans of 1850 show that Barry intended to retain the plaster ceiling of 1605; but in November 1851, Sir James wrote urgently to his wife: 'It will be necessary to have a new ceiling in the Dining Room. The present ceiling will fall on our heads.' Barry's design for the new plasterwork reproduced the old pattern in an enriched form, adding scrolls to the pendants and filling the panels with a 'KS' monogram within strapwork ribbing.

Left Crace curtains and wallpaper in the Dining Room

Crace furnishings

Wallpaper was supplied for the Dining Room in May 1852 by the decorating firm of J.G. Crace. The paper, later marketed as 'The Rutland', was printed in red flock to simulate the 16th-century Italian velvets from which the pattern is derived, but because of 'indifferent printing' (as the Clerk of Works described it), the pattern failed to match at the join. However, the paper was tolerated despite this disaster, and survived until the 1960s. In 1987 it was reprinted for this room using the original 'Rutland' blocks but with distempered colours.

The handsome 'Gothic tapestry' pattern for the wool and silk brocade curtains was devised by A.W.N. Pugin in 1844, inspired by 15th-century Italian figured silk velvets used as altar frontals. The present curtains have been reconstructed from surviving pieces of the 1852 originals, and re-hung on the brass rods which the Clerk of Works had anticipated 'Mr Crace would supply that there might be no mistake in the mode of hanging'.

The Dining Room

Above 'KS' monogram on
the Dining Room ceiling

Furniture

The room retains most of the furniture it
acquired in Victorian times. Some pieces were
supplied by J.G. Crace, such as the long trestle
table of Renaissance style. A design for the
top, showing the profile of its carved cornice
and frieze, has been found among the Barry
drawings, annotated 'tracing sent to Mr Crace
26th March 1852'.

The oak extending dining table on six
turned legs was made c.1881 by Gillows of
Lancaster, and the set of eighteen twist-
turned oak dining chairs may also be by
Gillows. This would have been a special order,
as the design of the chairs was taken from the
two existing 17th-century examples at either
end of the table. As most of their original
stamped velvet upholstery was removed some
time ago, the chairs have been re-covered in
new mohair velvet matching the old shade
of red and stamped with a pattern similar to
the original.

The carved oak 'Charles II' armchair with
attractively floral *petit point* embroidery in its
back and seat panels was made in Yorkshire in
the 1840s. Beside the chair is a mid-Victorian
trestle firescreen, its embroidered panel
worked in Berlin wools and silks on canvas,
with *petit point* details.

Regency lighting

When Robert Shuttleworth made this room
into the family Dining Room in 1816, he
ordered a magnificent six-branch oil lamp to
hang as a centrepiece. Using the latest
technology, it was of brightly burning Argand
type with cylindrical wicks and tall glass
chimneys to draw the air. The fuel was colza
oil, which because of its thick, viscous quality
was gravity-fed from a reservoir above –
ideally suited to a branched hanging lamp.
The lamp was made in 1817 by James DeVille
(d.1846), plaster figure maker and lamp
manufacturer, of 367 The Strand, London. Its
elegant Neo-classical design in bronze has
intricate gilt bronze mounts in the form of
lion masks, shells, and foliage, while a bronze
eagle alights on the domed cover of the
central reservoir. Sold from Gawthorpe in
1946, the lamp was repurchased in 2001 with
generous help from the Art Fund and the
Victoria & Albert Museum Purchase
Grant Fund.

Left The Dining Room in 1884; watercolour by N.E. Green

Portraits

Perhaps the finest of the National Portrait Gallery's portraits in this room is that of Sir Thomas Aylesbury, mathematician and stoical royalist, painted by William Dobson, c.1642. This hangs to the right of the fireplace. Three other portraits at the dais end of the room are of Civil War commanders: Spencer Compton, 2nd Earl of Northampton and his son Sir William Compton, both royalist heroes; and General George Monck, 1st Duke of Albemarle, a moderate Parliamentarian who led his army to restore Charles II. The portraits at either side of the screen are of James Harrington, a republican philosopher, and Nathaniel Highmore, a physician.

As in other rooms, the portraits are hung on cords rather than chains. The use of textile cords for hanging pictures was fashionable in the mid-19th century, and the Shuttleworth family portraits were hung in this way. Picture restorers Agnew's of Manchester, who re-gilded all the family picture frames in 1852, offered to supply Sir James Kay-Shuttleworth with cord which was dyed to the colour of the wallpaper.

Sculpture

Displayed on the long table are two alabaster models by Giuseppe Andreoni of Pisa; they represent two of the city's finest medieval buildings – the circular Baptistery and the church of Santa Maria della Spina. The models were bought in Italy by Blanche Kay-Shuttleworth in about 1880.

Carpet

The carpet is mid-19th-century, from the district of Feraghan in central Iran. Although not original to Gawthorpe, it is of the same date, style and manufacture as the one shown in the watercolour of 1884.

Below Alabaster model of Pisa Baptistery

The Drawing Room

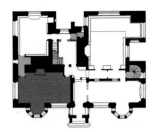

In 1605 this was known as the 'dyninge chamber', but in Robert Shuttleworth's reorganisation of rooms in 1816 it became the Drawing Room, a comfortable sitting room to which the family and guests might withdraw after their meal.

Listening to Sir James

The novelist Charlotte Brontë, who visited in March 1850, later recalled sitting here with Sir James, enjoying 'the dialogues (perhaps I should rather say monologues, for I listened far more than I talked) by the fireside in his antique oak-panelled drawing-room'.

Panelling and plasterwork

The room has always had the richest decoration in the house, and still retains its Jacobean panelling and plasterwork in remarkably good condition. The oak panelling, which took a year for three joiners to complete in 1603–4, is inlaid in the Italian Renaissance manner with attractive floral motifs set within carved arcading. Some carved and inlaid panels over the fireplace bear the date 1604 above the coat of arms of Lawrence Shuttleworth and the initials of his many relatives.

At intervals the cornice of the panelling breaks out to support the plaster statuary of the frieze, adding depth to a lively assemblage of figures entwined with fruiting stems and foliage. Vines and oak branches fill every available space in the strapwork of the ceiling. All this plasterwork is by the Yorkshire plasterers Francis and Thomas Gunby, and it occupied them for five months in the summer of 1605.

Decorative enrichment in Victorian times

Pugin designed the Gothic cast-iron fire grate with 'KS' monogram, furnished with a glorious pair of andirons bearing Kay-Shuttleworth armorial plates and exceptionally ornate finials of wrought brass. This complemented a rich and startlingly colourful furnishing scheme. The curtains shown in Victorian views of the room were probably supplied by Crace, and although the originals have gone, the material has been rewoven from a surviving fragment. It is a silk and linen brocatelle, in a bold pattern of stylised pomegranates and pineapples within strapwork.

In contrast to the bright green of the curtains, the original carpet was a lustrous blue and red Ziegler Mahal, with a distinctive character which its replacement retains. Another touch of colour was added c.1890 – the Venetian glass chandelier, one of a pair acquired for this room by Blanche Kay-Shuttleworth on one of her frequent visits to Italy.

Above Plaster statuary in the Drawing Room frieze

Below Plasterwork mermaid

The Drawing Room

Furniture by Pugin and Crace

All the principal furniture in this room was acquired in the 19th century, and much of it expresses the Victorians' wide-ranging antiquarian taste.

The centrepiece is an octagonal table designed by Pugin and manufactured by Crace. The top is of burr-walnut with an inlaid border of holly leaves and the Lancashire rose, on a Gothic trestle base of carved oak. A similar table was made c.1847 for the Prince's Chamber at the House of Lords, but there are few such tables in existence.

Keeping the tea safe

The highly decorative teapoy on a trestle stand contained the household tea caddies. Designed by Pugin, it has an exquisite inlaid pattern of flower chains and dog roses on its burr-walnut lid and front panel, and was made c.1850 as a special order for Janet Kay-Shuttleworth, whose monogram is carved into the rosewood trestle ends.

The pair of twin-hump settees, in buttoned velvet with deep fringes matching the curtains, has the square, chamfered legs characteristic of Pugin's furniture made by Gillows for the Houses of Parliament. One of the settees retains its 1850s green velvet, now dulled with age; the other, which at some time was re-upholstered in damask, has been re-covered in green velvet of the original brightness.

Antiquarian furniture

The set of twelve Dutch walnut chairs inlaid with marquetry was bought in 1851 by Sir James Kay-Shuttleworth – who, like many Victorians, would have seen nothing unusual in introducing this early 18th-century element into a Jacobean oak-panelled room. 'The Marqueterie Chairs look very well', he wrote to his wife in November 1851, 'and put our old furniture so much into the shade that we shall have to dismiss all the Drawing Room furniture and convert it to bedroom uses.' The antique dealer who supplied the chairs, together with a pair of matching pedestal tables, was William Sutcliffe, a Burnley cabinet-maker and upholsterer. It appears he had skilfully 'improved' the marquetry, reconstituting the chairs from an existing 18th-century set of 20 or more.

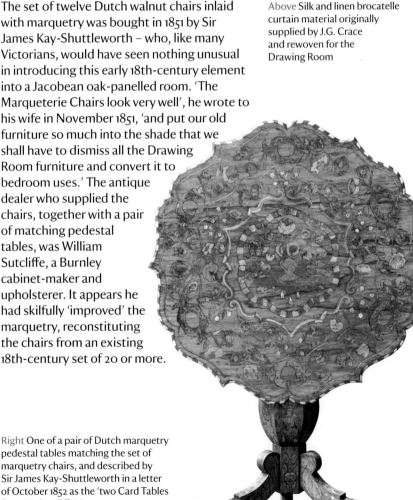

Above Silk and linen brocatelle curtain material originally supplied by J.G. Crace and rewoven for the Drawing Room

Right One of a pair of Dutch marquetry pedestal tables matching the set of marquetry chairs, and described by Sir James Kay-Shuttleworth in a letter of October 1852 as the 'two Card Tables from Mr Sutcliffe's'

Sir James referred to another of his purchases as 'the Elizabethan chairs made by Pratt'. These are identifiable as the two carved oak armchairs of 17th-century style. Samuel Luke Pratt was a London antique dealer who in 1854 described himself as a 'cabinet maker, importer of ancient furniture, armour &c.'. He specialised in making up this type of oak furniture, and may equally have been responsible for the two 'Jacobean' carved oak baluster stands in this room. Other Victorian reproductions of earlier styles include a Baroque mahogany child's chair and a 'Louis XIV' inlaid oval workbox.

In a class of its own is an extremely fine Louis XVI ebonised commode-cabinet with Japanese lacquer panels, marble top and gilt bronze mounts. This is by the French cabinet-maker Joseph Baumhauer (d.1772) and dates from c.1770. On it stand a mantel clock and pair of candelabra by Howell and James, c.1870. The clock, in gilt bronze case inset with onyx and supported on bronze sea-horses, was given to Ughtred and Blanche Kay-Shuttleworth as a wedding present in 1871 by the philanthropist Baroness Burdett-Coutts, who had it inscribed 'May the hand that holds the shuttle weave golden hours'. The couple duly celebrated their golden wedding anniversary in 1921.

Right Louis XVI ebonised commode, c.1770, with a clock and candelabra by Howell and James, c.1870

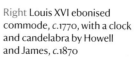

The Library
The Staircase

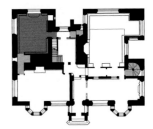

The Library
(occasional opening only)
This room was a small parlour until made into a library in 1816. It was refitted in 1850–52, and continues in use as the working library of the Textiles Collection.

The fireplace under a window is characteristic of Barry, although its stonework is undecorated. Barry is quoted as saying, 'The fire place is too small and low to admit of Shields in the Spandrels or the Motto in any part of it.' However, any decorative loss is made up by the massive stone doorcase, which has an intricately carved armorial panel dated 1851 with an appropriate motto, 'Literis Consiliis' (Be counselled by literature). Barry re-used the Regency mahogany door, and this may have been a cost-saver, but his linenfold panelling in the bookcase doors is a rare and perhaps costly indulgence in this Gothic feature.

In 1873, an attractive satin-ground flock paper was hung on panels near the door. It is the earliest known example of this paper by the French designer Paul Balin, complete with leather edging. The bookshelves now house Rachel Kay-Shuttleworth's books on textile crafts.

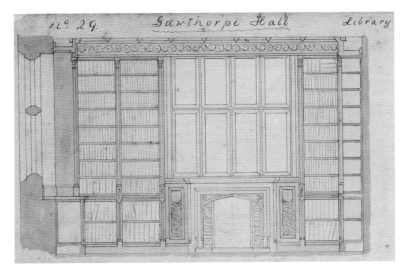

Above Detail from Charles Barry's plan and elevation of the Library, 1851

Right Carved stone panel over the door in the Library

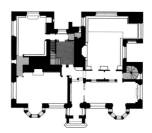

marble borders came from Knowles's marble works in Manchester, ready cut at 2s 6d per foot. Barry's first drawings for the woodwork show linenfold panelling, an elaborately carved balustrade, and heraldic figures on the newel posts. However, the design actually adopted was evidently a cheaper version, with plain panelling and peg-top balusters. At the same time, the windows were enlarged and fitted with the newly available luxury of plate glass.

Furniture and pictures

The longcase clock beside the large oak chest is of *c*.1775 by John Fletcher of Barnsley, using a brass dial of 1760 by Joseph Donisthorp of Normanton. In the mid-19th century, Fletcher's arched extension to the dial was painted with a rustic scene, and his oak case was embellished with carving.

Above the chest is hung a framed print, grandly entitled *The Central Executive, Cotton Famine Relief Committee, Manchester*. Sir James Kay-Shuttleworth was Vice-Chairman of this committee, which raised funds for the relief of unemployed cotton workers during the stoppage caused by the American Civil War. Three other prints on the staircase commemorate Queen Victoria's visit to Manchester in 1852.

The oil portraits on the first-floor landing are of Sir Ughtred and Lady Kay-Shuttleworth, painted in the Drawing Room in 1884 by the Hon. John Collier.

The Staircase

The present staircase of sandstone with oak balustrade is of 1850–2 and occupies three storeys of the tower. It supersedes a Neo-classical staircase of *c*.1816, which had replaced the original staircase of 1602–3.

The staircase hall is dominated by Barry's stone archways, built in a Perpendicular Gothic style reminiscent of the Houses of Parliament and decorated with the shields of the same heiresses as are featured in the Dining Room. Floor tiles were supplied in 1851 by Minton of Stoke-on-Trent, and laid in several different configurations using some of Pugin's Westminster patterns. The black

The Gawthorpe Textiles Collection

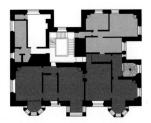

Most of the bedrooms, dressing rooms and passages on the first floor are now given over to displays of needlework, lace and associated items of costume collected by the Hon. Rachel Kay-Shuttleworth (1886–1967). The aim is to demonstrate the form and history of a wide range of techniques, as this was Rachel's main purpose in bringing the collection together. Her own creative talents were strongest in the field of embroidery and lace; she had an immense knowledge of needlecraft and was particularly concerned to teach others the traditional skills, through the medium of examples collected over a lifetime. These examples were not intended merely as museum pieces but as aids to practical study, and to inspire creativity.

Above Printed silk brocade bought in 1751 for a wedding dress

Treasures of embroidery, lace and costume

Rachel Kay-Shuttleworth's collection has continued to grow since her death in 1967, and now consists of more than 30,000 items. Traditional embroidery techniques are represented

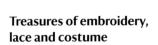

Above Sampler worked by Rachel Kay-Shuttleworth in the 1930s for use as a teaching aid when visiting workers' clubs to encourage women to take up embroidery during times of unemployment at the textile mills

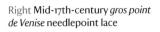

Right Mid-17th-century *gros point de Venise* needlepoint lace

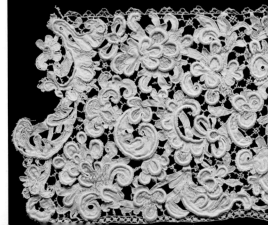

Left Rachel
Kay-Shuttleworth
with students in the
Drawing Room at
Gawthorpe in
the 1960s

by a wealth of examples ranging from samplers and canvaswork to exceptionally fine Ayrshire whitework and rare survivals of working smocks. The collection of patchwork quilts is unsurpassed in the richness and variety of its many documented examples. Numerous rare specimens of Mountmellick and Ruskin lace are to be found in the plentiful lace collection, while many examples of exotic needlework and costume, particularly from eastern countries, give the study of techniques a truly international dimension.

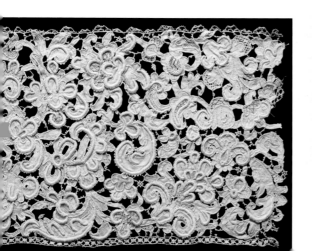

The Arts and Crafts movement

The greatest strength of Rachel's collection is in British needlework of her own time – the late 19th and early 20th centuries. The most significant items are those related to the Arts and Crafts movement. Rachel was a leading exponent of this revival of the vernacular tradition in embroidery, and she acquired an unparalleled collection of work produced by Arts and Crafts groups which had been set up to promote a renaissance in design and technical quality. The Royal School of Art Needlework, the Leek Embroidery Society, the Embroiderers' Guild and other pioneering groups are well represented, as are notable designers such as Edward Burne-Jones, Thomas Wardle and Lewis F. Day. In this area of work the Gawthorpe collection is the finest and most comprehensive of its kind outside the Victoria & Albert Museum.

The Gawthorpe Textiles Collection

The Passage and Boudoir

The passage from the Staircase is hung with framed embroidery, setting the scene for the main displays. The passage leads into the first of the exhibition rooms, in which artefacts and personal memorabilia of Rachel Kay-Shuttleworth provide an introduction to her life and work. The room was Rachel's 'boudoir' in the 1950s and '60s, and had been the private sitting room of the mistress of the house since at least 1852, when it was reported to have been hung with 'a very pretty green paper' for Rachel's grandmother, Janet Kay-Shuttleworth.

Below The Grey Room, one of the textiles galleries

The Bedrooms and Dressing Rooms

The second room – which was Janet's bedroom, decorated with 'a rich flock paper' – explores a number of themes from the astonishing variety of material in Rachel's collection. The design of the light oak showcases used throughout the exhibition reflects the spirit of the Arts and Crafts tradition which was such a strong influence on the artistic outlook of Rachel and her contemporaries. The cases were made locally in 1987 in the style of the Arts and Crafts architect and furniture designer C.F.A. Voysey (1857–1941).

The third room was referred to in 1850 as the Grey Room. It was decoratively plastered by Francis and Thomas Gunby in July 1604, and is believed to have been the bedchamber of the master of the house in Jacobean times. A plaque bearing the date 1604, with Lawrence Shuttleworth's initials below, can be seen above the 17th-century fireplace. In this room and the small room alongside, once the Grey Dressing Room, displays of Rachel's own work are complemented by some of the most fascinating pieces she collected.

Right Panel designed by William Morris, 1895, and worked by Rachel Kay-Shuttleworth's close friend Mrs R. Emma Day, wife of Lewis F. Day and a founder of the Embroiders' Guild

Above Book cover embroidered by Rachel Kay-Shuttleworth as a wedding present to her elder sister Nina in 1910. The honeysuckle flower is the Parish family crest, from their mother, Blanche Parish

The fifth and last of the exhibition rooms was Rachel's bedroom before the First World War, when it had a wallpaper of William Morris type. In 1850, when Barry's corner fireplace was installed, it was known as the Spotted Room, from an earlier decorative scheme. It still retains the neat geometrical ceiling put up by the Gunbys in 1604. Displays of needlework in this room are brought fully up to date with some lively examples of 20th- and 21st-century work from local communities, all inspired by pieces from Rachel Kay-Shuttleworth's collection.

The Family Exhibition

A changing exhibition of paintings, sculpture, photographs and memorabilia from the Shuttleworth family archive has been arranged in a former bedroom reached from a short passage off the first-floor landing.

Miss Rachel's 'Ark Room'

The room was created in 1908 by dividing a large bedroom, the new partition being given a cast of the Gunbys' plaster frieze which runs around the rest of the room. The passage was then hung with the wallpaper which still survives – a block print called 'Portuguese', manufactured in 1909 by Charles Knowles & Co. Later the room became Rachel Kay-Shuttleworth's 'Ark Room', containing the 'arks' or cupboards she used for storing textiles. The printed cotton of the curtains and settee cover replicates a Pugin-style fabric printed in Lancashire in 1861 for J.G. Crace and used at Gawthorpe for case covers.

Pictures and sculpture

Among the pictures is a charming but anonymous oil painting of Blanche Kay-Shuttleworth in the Drawing Room with her baby daughter Angela, *c*.1873. It accompanies two interior watercolours and a triptych of exteriors, all painted in 1884 by Nathaniel Everett Green (1823–99), an art teacher to the royal family. A pair of cameo portraits in alabaster, sculpted by Alexander Carrick in 1921, commemorates Lawrence and Edward Kay-Shuttleworth, the two brothers who were killed in the First World War. Two further posthumous portraits, by Harold Speed, are hung in the passage. These are of the 2nd and 3rd Lords Shuttleworth, both killed in the Second World War.

Below Blanche Kay-Shuttleworth with her daughter in the Drawing Room; by an unknown artist, *c*.1873

The Long Gallery

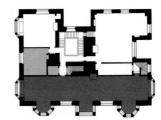

Over 70 feet (21 metres) in length, the Long Gallery takes up the entire south front at second-floor level. It is decorated and furnished as it might have appeared in the 1850s, and yet retains the plasterwork and indeed the whole architectural purpose of an early 17th-century long gallery, in which the family and guests could walk up and down at leisure and review the portraits of ancestors and great figures from the past. Today's visitors have the chance to see portraits from the National Portrait Gallery's collection, featuring some of the most colourful characters in the social and political life of 17th-century England.

Decoration

Francis and Thomas Gunby completed the plaster fretwork ceiling in 1603. It was the year of James I's accession, and their overmantel to the fireplace carries the new King's coat of arms with the crown and garter, flanked by male and female supporters above a panel of pious maxims in English and Latin. A Pugin-style fire grate was installed in the 1850s, but the tiles, probably by William De Morgan, are of c.1890.

New doorcases were fitted in 1852, when the walls were hung with a rich flock paper designed by Pugin. The flock paper was later destroyed but has been recreated from samples found behind the doorcases. It has a

Above The Long Gallery

bold strapwork pattern of thistles and other flowers on a ground of ginger flock, picked out in gold leaf and maroon flock on a vellum ground. The design is inspired by Italian Renaissance brocades, and would have shimmered in candlelight.

Furniture

Oak furniture is ranged around the walls in the formal 17th-century manner which was fashionable in the 1840s and '50s, when these pieces were acquired from dealers' workshops. The 'Elizabethan' court cupboard to the right of the fireplace is a pyramid of three unrelated cupboards ingeniously unified by applied carving. A similar composition to the left has a handsome three-tier press cupboard of 1596 unhappily balanced on a later spindle-fronted cupboard, with carving to mask the join. The cupboards are attended by two sets of high-backed 'Charles II' chairs, equally 'made-up' but of commendable quality.

The longcase clock at the end of the room has a lantern clock movement of c.1700 in a carved oak case, rather improbably dated 1654. The case was made up by Samuel Pratt of London, whose 'Elizabethan' chairs in the Drawing Room have the same pair of crudely carved cherubs bearing a crown.

Portraits from the National Portrait Gallery

Leaders of society in the second half of the 17th century – both at Court and in the literary world – are well represented in this distinguished gathering. To the right of the fireplace are a version of Lely's Duchess of Cleveland (Charles II's mistress) and J.M. Wright's state portrait of Charles II, in an exceptionally elaborate frame. Two small portraits of William Chiffinch and the diarist Samuel Pepys hang opposite, in company with a magnificent full-length of the Earl of Oxford by Kneller. Half-lengths of Monmouth, Clarendon, John Locke and Robert Boyle occupy smaller spaces, and at the far end of the room is another, equally grand, full-length by Kneller of the Earl of Rochester. The remaining four portraits, on the fireplace wall, are three-quarter-lengths of writers: the pamphleteer Eleanor James, wearing fine lace of c.1690; the poet Abraham Cowley, by Lely; the political commentator Sir Roger L'Estrange, by J.M. Wright; and the dramatist Thomas Killigrew, in a famous portrait by William Sheppard.

Top left Plaster overmantel in the Long Gallery dated 1603

Above A longcase clock from the Shuttleworths' collection of early Victorian oak furniture

Left *Portrait of Charles II*; by J.M. Wright, c.1660 (National Portrait Gallery)

The Huntroyde Room

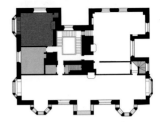

Always the best bedroom, this room has been known by several different names. The 1st Lord Shuttleworth gave it the name Huntroyde Room, from its view of the neighbouring estate of Huntroyde.

Decoration
The plaster decoration of 1604 by the Gunby partnership has a significantly greater richness than any other bedroom, particularly in the overmantel, with its vigorous rendering of the Shuttleworth coat of arms supported by two female figures representing Prudence and Justice, from the family motto. The wallpaper replicates the room's earliest known paper – a block-print of 1894 by Jeffrey & Co. The design is called 'Lily and Rose', by the Pre-Raphaelite artist Walter Crane, who papered his own dining room with the same pattern.

Furniture
The carved oak tester bed, dated 1650, is a skilful blend of various 17th-century components and some Victorian additions. Rachel Kay-Shuttleworth embroidered the crewel-work 'Tree of Life' bed hangings and counterpane, inspired by the many Jacobean floral motifs and coats of arms to be seen at Gawthorpe. The work took her many years to complete, and on Armistice Day 1918 she recorded the date on the upper valance, with a palm tree to celebrate Peace.

Gothic Revival carving on the table mirror and washstand betrays the same early Victorian origins as the bed. The large Italian cassone or clothes chest, opposite the bed, may also be a 19th-century piece, although of a type produced in the mid-15th century. Such chests are decorated on the top with armorials in painted and gilded plaster, and on the front with biblical or mythological scenes; this one depicts St George and the Dragon.

Pictures
More portraits from the National Portrait Gallery hang in this room. The large portrait to the left of the window bay is of Marie-Anne Mancini, Duchess of Bouillon, painted in 1673 by Benedetto Gennari. She is portrayed as Cleopatra in richly brocaded robes. A small portrait to the left is of another Italian beauty, once thought to be Anne-Marie's sister, Hortense Mancini, Duchess of Mazarin, a mistress of Charles II.

Left Plaster overmantel in the Huntroyde Room

Above Crewel-work 'Tree of Life' bed hanging embroidered by Rachel Kay-Shuttleworth, 1910–18

Left
The Huntroyde Room

A 1690s portrait of Daniel Purcell, brother of the famous composer, hangs to the left of the bed. The portrait opposite the door, in a rare mid-17th-century frame ornamented with gilt papier mâché, is traditionally said to be of Elizabeth, Princess Palatine, sister of Charles I.

The exotic flower picture hanging to the right of the fireplace and entitled *Japan* is by Marianne North (1830–90), intrepid traveller and painter of botanical subjects. Marianne North was one of Janet Shuttleworth's half-sisters and a frequent visitor to Gawthorpe. She was known to Janet's children as 'Aunt Pop'.

Ceramics

On either side of the fireplace hangs a pair of framed Italian maiolica plates from Castelli, painted with landscapes in metallic lustre pigments and gilding. The landscapes are attributed to the early 18th-century painter Luigi Grue.

Textiles

The window curtains and pelmets, of linen and crewel work, were embroidered in the 1940s by Mrs Dora Morse of Claughton Hall, Lancaster, for her daughter, Mrs Mary Barton, a close friend of Rachel Kay-Shuttleworth.

The Garden

The Gawthorpe estate in medieval times was a small agricultural settlement on which arable land was cultivated within the royal Forest of Pendle. During the Tudor period, the Shuttleworth family increased their holdings considerably, such that by 1600 it was a highly prosperous estate which financed the building of Gawthorpe Hall, with its significantly capacious Great Barn. The earliest surviving picture of the Hall (illustrated below) shows a garden of formal 17th-century style at the front of the house. Stone walls enclose a neat arrangement of long rectangular flower-beds meticulously planted with rows of white and red flowers.

Left South view of Gawthorpe Hall and its formal garden in the early 18th century. Painting attributed to Leonard Knyff (1650–1721)

Left South view of
Gawthorpe Hall in
1884. Watercolour by
N.E. Green

Loss and revival of formality

By about 1816 the old formal garden had been
swept away and replaced by a carriage drive to
the front door. It was probably Robert
Shuttleworth (d.1818) who created the open
landscape shown in early 19th-century views.
In the 1840s, Robert's daughter Janet and her
husband Sir James Kay-Shuttleworth built a
stone balustraded terrace at the back of the
house. This heralded the restoration of a
formal garden in the 1850s as part of the work
of the architect Sir Charles Barry.

In the words of Barry's son Alfred, he
'carried out the same principle of architectural
gardening, which he had so often exemplified
in his Italian buildings, by surrounding the
house with a formal garden, designed
according to the geometrical patterns of the
Elizabethan period'. To make room for this,
Barry extended the level area at the south
front of the house by excavating the slope,
and used the waste material to form an
enlarged, semicircular 'bastion' at the back of
the house, extending the 1840s terrace
northwards to create a wider view towards
Pendle Hill. He then devised elaborate
parterres consisting of gravel paths and
flower-beds, which could be seen to best
effect from the upper windows.

Right Detail from an
estate map of c.1816,
with a walled garden
between the Hall and
the Estate Building.
The bed of the River
Calder is shown, but
the river had been
diverted because of
pollution and was not
moved back until 1960

The Victorian heyday of the Garden

Community gardening

The parterres were largely completed in 1852, but flights of steps and angular stone urns faceted with Pugin's Westminster tiles were still at the drawing-board stage in 1856 and may not have been set up until 1862, by then providing work for unemployed mill operatives during the Cotton Famine. The flower-beds were planted with masses of showy and colourful flowers like dahlias, chrysanthemums and carnations, with clusters of smaller plants forming patterns around specimen yuccas. All was kept in perfect order by Thomas Birtwell the Head Gardener, assisted by four under-gardeners and a boy apprentice.

Members of the public were allowed access to the garden at a surprisingly early date. About 1860, as the 1st Lord Shuttleworth later recalled, Sir James Kay-Shuttleworth 'decided, not without some anxious protests from at least one neighbouring clergyman, to throw open the grounds at Gawthorpe to the public for three or four hours on Sunday afternoons'. Such was its popularity that the Sunday opening became a permanent institution. Sir James was often to be seen enjoying a stroll among the visitors, chatting with some of them, and only occasionally having to correct unmannerly behaviour.

The North Parterre

Charles Barry's radial parterre, with its shaped stone kerbs, gravel paths and stone parapet spiked with obelisks, has largely survived intact. The beds are planted with blocks of golden privet, edged with dwarf purple-leaved berberis and punctuated with 'dots' of common privet and *Yucca gloriosa*. The outlying domes are *Lonicera nitida* 'Baggesen's Gold'. Armorial stone seats of Elizabethan style designed by Barry's son Edward are to be found at either end of the long terrace.

Right **The North Parterre**

The Walled Garden

On higher ground to the east of the Hall is an early 19th-century walled kitchen garden which was dramatically improved in the 1870s with a number of new vineries, and hot-houses producing exotic fruit. A heated grotto for ferns was an intriguing feature added in the 1890s. The walled garden is now derelict, but could in time be restored.

The Woodland

Remnants of ancient oakwood may have survived into the 19th century, but were then diversified to produce what is now a mixture of native hardwood trees and a few ornamental conifers. In August 1876 Ughtred Kay-Shuttleworth reported to his father that 'the thinning of trees in the grounds has answered well & we are getting individual trees & groups, of beautiful form and foliage, as the crowding diminishes & the poor old oaks by degrees make room for the beeches, limes, elms &c.'. Some of Ughtred's hardwoods were later lost to disease, or to the ravages of open-cast coal mining in the 1950s, but the present woodland of 16ha (40 acres) is gradually being restored to its Victorian character.

The Drives

Gawthorpe's two drives, leading from lodge gates a mile apart on the Burnley Road, converge as they approach the front of the house. The Stockbridge Drive, from Padiham, has an Elizabethan-style lodge of 1852 by Barry. The longer Habergham Drive starts from Habergham Eaves, near the church of All Saints, which was built jointly by the Kay-Shuttleworth and Dugdale families in 1846–9. This drive was made in 1862, employing gangs of laid-off cotton workers, and its lodge is another Elizabethan eye-catcher of Barry design.

Below left Barry's drawing for a finial on the semicircular parapet of the North Parterre

Below right Barry's parterre of strapwork design in the South Garden, photographed c.1900. It was made into a lawn in the 1960s, but could in time be recreated

The Estate Yard

The Great Barn

Larger than the Hall itself, this spectacular 30m (100ft) aisled barn of 1603–5 is an important survival of a type uncommon in Lancashire. Aisled barns provided much greater width than the normal cruck-framed barn in order to accommodate cattle and farm equipment in addition to enormous quantities of grain, straw and animal feed. Lofty stone-based aisle posts carry both the arcade plate (the main horizontal timber supporting the roof) and the tie-beams of the principal rafters. Elegant curved bracing gives the whole structure a cathedral-like quality.

Account books identify two masons, William and John Whithead, as the building contractors. Foundations were laid in April 1603, and by August 1604 the walls were complete and the roof timbers in place. Work continued until the end of 1605, with flagstones laid as a threshing floor between the two opposed wagon entrances, and timbering erected for an oxen house in the south-east aisle, complete with paved dung passage and loft above. In Victorian times, the two southernmost bays of this 9-bay barn were converted into stables, the gable end being pierced by arched doorways, mullioned windows and a loading door for the hay loft. More recent improvements such as the installation of lighting and underfloor heating have retained the character of the building while making the interior a versatile space for events.

Left South gable end of the Great Barn, with the coach house adjoining

Right Interior of the Great Barn in 1999, when in use for an exhibition of work by the sculptor David Nash

The Coach House

Built onto a corner of the Great Barn in 1870, the coach house has arched gateways, a hipped roof and corbelling at the eaves which suggest a military Gothic style which is not otherwise seen at Gawthorpe. Vehicles kept here in the 1870s included a brougham, an open carriage, a dog cart, and a ladies' pony carriage. It is now used as a tea-room.

The Estate Building

The two-storey, L-shaped range known as the Estate Building is mostly 17th-century. The earliest part is the stable in the south-east angle, built in 1605–6. The upper floor was once a hay loft, with massive roof trusses. The largest of the first-floor rooms in the east range was formerly the estate office, and this too has prodigious roof timbers. Apartments below and at either end of the estate office were occupied by estate staff: coachman, grooms, under-gardeners, gamekeeper and carter. In the south range, a harness room adjoined the stable, and beyond that was the laundry. Refitted in 1876, it was operated by a washerwoman and her two daughters who lived over the wash-house. When the family was away, the laundry would arrive by train each week in huge baskets collected from the station by the carter. In 1922, an old coach house at the end of this wing became the garage for a Rolls-Royce.

Building the Hall

The design of Gawthorpe Hall is attributed on stylistic grounds to Robert Smythson (c.1535–1614), architect of Wollaton Hall in Nottinghamshire, Hardwick Hall in Derbyshire and numerous other Elizabethan houses to be found mostly in the north Midlands and south Yorkshire. Smythson's hand is apparent in all the principal features: the tall, compact entrance front of three projecting bays, generously endowed with mullioned windows; the staircase tower, pinnacled with chimneystacks and containing a prospect room looking out over the countryside; and the ingenious arrangement of the interior, in which the great hall is placed unusually along the side of the house, and the domestic offices are relegated to the basement.

Smythson is likely to have supplied a plan, with elevations of the symmetrical south and west fronts, leaving the execution and detailing to local builders. The Rev. Lawrence Shuttleworth's account books provide much information about the progress of the work, the materials used, and the names and wages of the workmen. From February to June 1600, sandstone was quarried at Gawthorpe and on other Shuttleworth lands nearby, and timber was bought, felled and transported from Mitton Wood, near Whalley. When the first stone was laid, on 26 August, all the workmen and household servants were given a pair of gloves.

Building work was supervised by the chief mason, Anthony Whithead (d.1608) of

Above Plaster panel in the ceiling of the Huntroyde Room

Emmott near Colne, who was retained on a high salary of 30 shillings a quarter. His particular importance was that he acted as a surveyor, and may have produced working drawings from plans provided by the architect. Among the more highly paid of the contractors was Henry Mylner, the chief 'wright' or carpenter, on a daily rate of 5d and later 6d. Other masons, wallers and wrights averaged 4d a day, apprentices and servants 3d or 2d, and unskilled labourers, 1d. In

addition, free board and lodging was made available in houses nearby.

An older hall, in which Lawrence Shuttleworth occupied the 'master's chamber' during his frequent visits, must have existed at Gawthorpe, although its location is unknown. There is a tradition that a medieval tower house was incorporated into the new building, but the accounts give no evidence for this. The new building had reached its full height by June 1602, when the roof was laid and a piper was paid 6d to help celebrate the 'Rearinge day'.

Above The earliest view of Gawthorpe Hall. Detail from an early 18th-century painting attributed to Leonard Knyff

Left Carved oak panelling above the fireplace in the Drawing Room, showing the Shuttleworth coat of arms

Building the Hall

Jacobean craftsmen

For four years from 1602, gangs of joiners, plasterers and other craftsmen were engaged in fitting out, decorating and furnishing the interior. The joiners panelled all the ground-floor rooms in 1603–4, with the decorative carved and inlaid work being done by Thomas Hurdeys, Hugh Sandes and an apprentice, Cornelius Towndley. The highest paid of the joiners was Thomas Hurdeys, at 6d a day, and he also undertook stone-carving.

The plasterers started in the Long Gallery in 1603, moving down to the first-floor bedchambers in 1604. They then followed the joiners into the ground-floor rooms, finishing in 1605 with the ceilings and friezes of the panelled dining chamber and great hall (now Drawing Room and Dining Room). This enabled them to use the top of the panelling for plaster statuary in the frieze.

Decorative plasterwork was undertaken by Francis and Thomas Gunby, of whom the more highly skilled was Francis, on 6d a day; he was responsible for cutting the moulds, and was at first described as a joiner. The Gunbys were based in West Yorkshire, where they had worked on houses for Sir John Savile in the 1580s. They reused at least one Savile frieze ornament at Gawthorpe, and while they did make some moulds for Gawthorpe, they reused various others. There are at least six West Yorkshire houses with an example of a Gunby plaster ornament also found in ceilings or friezes at Gawthorpe.

The first occupant of the Hall was probably Lawrence Shuttleworth's nephew Richard, who lived at Gawthorpe until his death in 1669; but thereafter the Shuttleworths tended to live elsewhere, allowing the house to remain unaltered throughout the 18th century.

Above Gawthorpe Hall Wainscot Room, as sketched by Charles Barry junior in February 1850 before it was dismantled. The ceiling roses contained the mottoes *God save our King and Queen* and *God defend us from Turke and Pope*. All the oak furniture has survived; the chair can be seen in the Long Gallery, the bed and table mirror in the Huntroyde Room

Left Heraldic plaster figure above the panelling in the Drawing Room

Regency repairs

In 1816 the house was inherited by Robert Shuttleworth (1784–1818), who immediately embarked upon repairs and alterations in a Neo-classical style. He demolished the Jacobean oak staircase and erected a Regency one, and refitted a small parlour to create a library; of his work nothing now remains except a few six-panelled doors of figured mahogany.

Sir Charles Barry

In 1850–52, a far more radical programme of repairs and improvements was carried out for Robert's son-in-law, Sir James Kay-Shuttleworth. The architect he commissioned in April 1849 was Sir Charles Barry (1795–1860), famed as the architect of the Palace of Westminster and a number of country houses in various Italianate or late Gothic styles. At Gawthorpe, Barry worked exclusively in an Elizabethan style, intending any new work to enhance the old.

Barry raised the staircase tower by one storey, adding openwork parapets of hard freestone from Catlow (a local quarry), while surrounding the house with a ground-level balustrade to provide a frame for the exterior, and imposing further uniformity by tidying up some window levels on the rear elevations. He also heightened Smythson's front porch to accommodate an outer door with a window above, so that it out-topped the ground-floor windows – an alteration at the request of Sir James, but studiously avoided in Barry's early drawings.

In the house, Barry swept away the incongruous Regency staircase and replaced it with one of Elizabethan style, panelled in oak. Sir James wrote to his wife in February 1851: '[Mr. Barry] wishes me to pannel the whole of the walls of the Staircase as he then thinks the interior of the house will have an even more Elizabethan character.' In creating a new Entrance Hall, Barry had to dismantle a Jacobean mezzanine bedroom called the Wainscot Room, managing to preserve only a few panels and an inlaid overmantel for reuse.

All the main contractors were locally based, like William Horne of Padiham, the principal joiner, and William and James Duckett of Burnley, the partnership responsible for most of the building work. One mason, however, had been employed on other Barry commissions, having worked at the Houses of Parliament for four years at a good rate of 5s a day; but in moving north to Gawthorpe he was able to earn only 4s a day.

Above
Sir Charles Barry
1859–60 (National Portrait Gallery)

'When Mr. Barry was consulted by Sir James P. K. Shuttleworth, in 1849, he felt unwilling to make any considerable alterations. All he thought needful was to give importance to the tower and chimneys, by raising them so as to produce greater boldness in the sky-line, and to surround the building with a pierced parapet of the characteristic Elizabethan style. The changes were not great, but they all tended to perfect and render more striking the original character of the building.'

Charles Barry's son Alfred, writing in c.1867

Left
Barry's contract drawing for the South Front, dated January 1850, with proposed new work shown in colour wash

Building the Hall

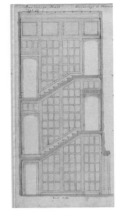

Above Detail from
Barry's drawing for the
staircase panelling as
built, 1851

Gawthorpe transformed

The restoration work of 1850–52 is fully documented in Barry's architectural drawings and in the letters of F.H. Groves, the London surveyor whom Sir James had appointed as clerk of works at a salary of 3 guineas a week. In reports sent regularly to Sir James in London, Groves provides a fascinating commentary on the work done and the problems encountered. He records, for instance, how the base of the tower was found to have been 'sadly mangled from time to time' and had to be massively buttressed. Afterwards he coolly remarks upon 'the narrow escape we have had of raising the Tower upon a most unsound foundation.'

Throughout the house, many timbers were found to have decayed, such that some decorative ceilings had to be renewed, as in the Dining Room and Library, or skilfully repaired, as in the 'Buff Room' (the later Huntroyde Room) and the Long Gallery. Some old oak floors had acquired a slope because of early settlement in the tower, and new pitch pine flooring was laid on top to make them level – so as not to be 'a source of annoyance in the standing of the Furniture', as Groves put it.

Few structural changes were made to the Hall after Barry's time – the one major reversal of his work being the conversion of the Entrance Hall into a kitchen in 1945. The Entrance Hall was reinstated by the National Trust in 1986–7, when the principal rooms were returned as nearly as possible to their appearance in Victorian times, using the abundant documentary evidence to recreate one of the richest periods in the history of the house.

Right Inlaid walnut and rosewood teapoy designed by Pugin for Janet Kay-Shuttleworth, c.1850

Refurnishing the rooms

The most significant contributions to refurnishing in the 1850s came from the architect and furniture designer A.W.N. Pugin (1812–52) and the interior decorator J.G. Crace (1809–89). These leading lights of the Gothic Revival collaborated with Barry on the Houses of Parliament; but they are not known to have worked with him on any country house except Gawthorpe.

Pugin supplied designs to Crace for making up Gothic furniture in inlaid walnut and oak, and to the ironwork manufacturer John Hardman of Birmingham for Gothic fire grates and the ironwork for the front door. Crace's interior decorating firm also supplied carpets, curtains and wallpapers, some of which were Pugin designs from previous commissions. The floor tiles chosen and arranged by Barry were made by Minton of Stoke-on-Trent in various patterns devised by Pugin for the Houses of Parliament.

Grand designs

Barry's first proposals for enhancing the interior were beautifully elaborate but scarcely affordable. The Staircase was to have rich carving on the panelling and balustrade, with heraldic figures on the newel posts, while the Dining Room was to have panels carved in a linenfold pattern – a feature also proposed for the Entrance Hall, where the panelling was to be surmounted by a row of fitted portraits. None of this elaboration was executed. Another of Barry's proposals was to have heraldic carved stone panels on the exterior, above and below the windows of the south front; but after much haggling over estimates, the idea was regretfully abandoned.

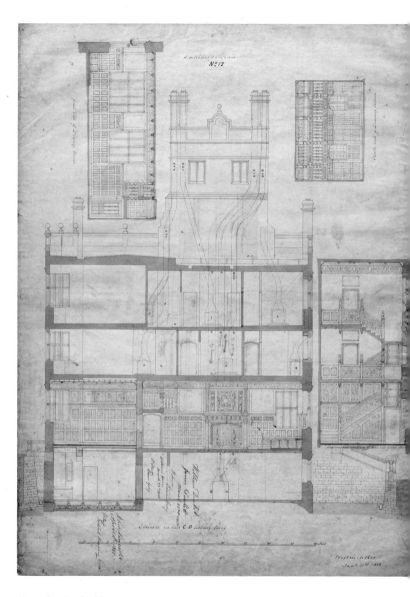

Above Section looking west, dated January 1850, showing Barry's first proposals for the interior. The drawing also shows cross-sections of the Dining Room ceiling and minstrels' gallery in their original form, prior to alterations by Barry

The Shuttleworth Family

From medieval origins to Tudor prosperity

The first of the Shuttleworth family to be recorded as owning land at Gawthorpe was Ughtred de Shuttleworth in 1388. Ughtred, whose name is a medieval variant of Hugh, was a younger son of Henry de Shuttleworth of Shuttleworth Hall, Hapton, near Padiham, and Agnes, daughter and heiress of William de Hacking of Hacking Hall, near Whalley. He therefore belonged to the landed gentry of the area, and bore a coat of arms of three weaver's shuttles. The family name and crest might suggest an involvement in woollen manufacturing, but there is no evidence for this.

Ughtred's descendants made various useful marriage alliances with landed families, greatly increasing the wealth and social standing of the Shuttleworths. His grandson Lawrence married Elizabeth Worsley, who inherited an estate at Twiston in Lancashire, and his great grandson Nicholas married Ellen, daughter of Christopher Parker of Radholme Park, near Clitheroe. Nicholas's wife was the cousin of Edmund Parker who built Browsholme Hall in 1507, and his brother and two sisters married into the eminent Lancashire families of Towneley, Cunliffe and Talbot. In 1540, Nicholas's son Hugh married Anne Grimshaw of Clayton Hall, Clayton-le-Moors.

The family recorded in 1604

Five generations of Shuttleworths are commemorated by initials and dates in an inlaid oak panel devised by the Rev. Lawrence Shuttleworth.

Top row: (left) Lawrence Shuttleworth (b.1443) and his wife Elizabeth; **(right)** their son Nicholas (b.1473) and his wife Ellen.

Second row: (left) Nicholas and Ellen's son Hugh and his wife Anne, with 1577 as Hugh's acceptance of the Protestant faith in advance of anti-Catholic legislation; **(right)** Hugh and Anne's eldest son Sir Richard (d.1599), recorded as 'K[night] S[epultus] 1599'.

Third row: (left) Sir Richard's younger brother Lawrence (b.1545), recorded as 'P[resbyter] N[atus] 1545'; **(right)** Lawrence's younger brother Thomas and his wife Anne (m.1586).

Bottom row: Richard, Nicholas and Ughtred Shuttleworth, the three sons of Thomas and Anne, in 1604.

A fortune made and spent

Much of the Shuttleworth family fortune was accumulated in Elizabethan times by Hugh's eldest son, Sir Richard Shuttleworth (c.1541–99), a London barrister who became a Serjeant at Law in 1584 and Chief Justice of Chester in 1589. From the profits of the legal profession he purchased estates at Barbon in Westmorland, Inskip in West Lancashire and Forcett and Austwick in North Yorkshire. He made his home at Smithills Hall, near Bolton, which he held in right of his wife, Margery, widow of Robert Barton of Smithills. His legal right to Smithills came to an end with his wife's death in 1592, and when his father died in 1596, Sir Richard may have laid plans for the new building at Gawthorpe. However, he died in 1599, leaving the project to be carried into effect by his younger brother, the Rev. Lawrence Shuttleworth (1545–1608), who since 1582 had been Rector of Whichford in Warwickshire.

The Rev. Lawrence, or 'Mr parson Shuttleworth', as a neighbour referred to him in 1602, was businesslike and puritanical. He visited Gawthorpe regularly to oversee the building work, but probably never lived at the Hall, as it was scarcely completed when he died in 1608. He never married; but fortunately there were six children of the marriage of his younger brother Thomas (1546–93) and Anne Lever of Little Lever, near Bolton.

Richard, later Colonel, Shuttleworth (1587–1669), eldest son of Thomas, inherited the newly-built Gawthorpe Hall in February 1608 and shortly afterwards married Fleetwood, daughter and heiress of Richard Barton of Barton Lodge, near Preston. This was a particularly rich and colourful period in the social history of Gawthorpe. Richard was very much a patron of the performing arts. In the decade 1610–20 he hired various companies of players to put on plays in the great hall, and dozens of other artists ranging from musicians to circus entertainers. In August 1612 he paid Lord Monteagle's players the considerable sum of 50s on one occasion (possibly to celebrate the birth of an heir), and later he paid Lord Stafford's and Lord Dudley's players 40s and 30s respectively, and Lord Derby's players 34s for two appearances. Patronage on this scale was exercised by relatively few families in Lancashire at that period.

Top left The Rev. Lawrence Shuttleworth (1545–1608). By an unknown artist, 1600

Bottom left Col. Richard Shuttleworth (1587–1669). By an unknown artist, c.1610

The Shuttleworth Family

Above
Col. Richard Shuttleworth
(1587–1669). By an unknown
artist, c.1650

The 17th and 18th centuries

The Civil War and Restoration

Col. Richard Shuttleworth (1587–1669) was
High Sheriff of Lancashire twice, and MP for
Preston from 1641. At the outbreak of Civil War
in 1642, he was appointed colonel of
Parliamentary forces in north-east Lancashire.
Five of his sons took up arms for Parliament;
and one of them, William, a 20-year-old
captain, was killed at the gates of Lancaster
castle in March 1643, following the capture of
the town by royalists under the Earl of Derby.
A month later, Derby's forces were about five
miles from Gawthorpe when Colonel
Shuttleworth's men under Captain Ashton
marched out and defeated the royalists in a
skirmish which became known as the Battle of
Whalley. The action not only saved Gawthorpe
from capture but also hastened the royalist
collapse throughout Lancashire.

The Colonel's rigorous administration as a
magistrate and sequestrator of the estates of
'delinquent' royalists, and more especially his
Presbyterian zeal as an ecclesiastical
commissioner during the Commonwealth,
caused bitter resentment among royalists and
churchmen. One of his official duties as a
Justice of the Peace in the 1650s was the
solemnization of marriages, many of which
were held at Gawthorpe. However, he later
admitted that his mistress (or 'second wife')
Judith Thorpe had borne the last nine of his
eleven children. Locally nicknamed 'Old

Above ?Capt. William Shuttleworth (d.1643).
Style of Robert Walker, painted
posthumously, c.1650

Politics and pleasure in the 18th century

Richard 'Ready Money Dick' Shuttleworth (1683–1749) succeeded his father Sir Richard at the age of four, and became Tory MP for Lancashire at the age of 22. He served in ten Parliaments, eventually becoming Father of the House. His son James (1714–73) was Tory MP for Preston from 1741 and for Lancashire from 1761. Both lived at Forcett, and in 1760 James was High Sheriff of Yorkshire. Gawthorpe meanwhile was let to Alexander Nowell (1682–1748), and later to his son Ralph (1721–80), of Read Hall. The Nowells were a staunch royalist family who allegedly supported the Jacobites in 1745 – as was perhaps substantiated by the discovery in 1850 of a hoard of gold coins from that time, hastily deposited under a windowsill at Gawthorpe.

The owner of Gawthorpe in the late 18th century was Robert Shuttleworth (c.1745–1816), eldest son of James Shuttleworth and his wife Mary Holden, an heiress, of Aston Hall in Derbyshire. Robert married Anne, daughter of George III's equerry, General Desaguliers, and lived a life of luxury in southern England. He sold the Yorkshire estates (partly to finance a passion for yachts) and in 1792 bought an estate on Prince Edward Island, Canada. There he was hailed as 'a gentleman of great opulence' who brought with him not only his family and furniture but 'likewise a master-carpenter to superintend the building of a large and elegant Mansion House'. Robert's colonial adventure lasted only two years, however, and he sold the Canadian estate in 1804. In his time, Gawthorpe Hall is said to have been occupied by a steward called Whyman, who treated it as a farmhouse.

Below Richard Shuttleworth (1683–1749), called 'Ready Money Dick'; by John Vanderbank, 1722

Smoot', this smooth-tongued politician survived well into the Restoration era. He left his estates to his grandson Richard, son of his (legitimate) eldest son, Colonel Richard the younger, who had been MP for Clitheroe from 1640 until his early death in 1648.

Richard Shuttleworth (1644–81) had been brought up at Forcett in Yorkshire and continued to live there in the 1670s with his wife Margaret, daughter of the royalist John Tempest of Old Durham. Twice High Sheriff of Yorkshire, Richard was only 36 when he died. His young son, another Richard (1666–87), married in 1682 a 15-year-old heiress, Catherine Clerke (nicknamed 'The Infanta'), daughter of the President of Magdalen College, Oxford. Tragically, three years after he had been knighted by Charles II, Sir Richard died at the age of 21, at Gawthorpe, where his father-in-law had died a few weeks earlier. After this double bereavement the house was not lived in by the Shuttleworths for three generations.

The Shuttleworth Family

The 19th century

The return to Gawthorpe

Robert Shuttleworth (1784–1818) became a barrister and chairman of Quarter Sessions at Preston, where his enlightened approach earned him the epithet 'The People's Magistrate'. Early in 1816 he made Gawthorpe his home and began repairs and improvements. In November he married Janet Marjoribanks, daughter of a Scottish baronet; but in March 1818 he died after a carriage accident, leaving a daughter, Janet, only four months old.

The heiress Janet Shuttleworth was brought up in the south and did not live at Gawthorpe until after her marriage in 1842. During a short visit in 1836, she wrote in her diary: 'Dear old Gawthorpe is in full beauty. We are full of plans for papering, painting and repairing this dear old place – a great deal is required to put it in good order for a constant residence, and this I hope in time to be able to do, and to make it my abode. The tiresome thing is that it is not considered proprietous for a young lady to live alone in her own house.' Towards the end of her stay, she added: 'Mary Smith [the laundry-maid] has been here to take leave of me to-day and advising me to marry and "be sure and get a good man, Miss, who'll be like to live here".' Six years later she married Dr James Phillips Kay, the celebrated Victorian educationalist, now regarded as the founder of public education in this country.

Rewarded with a baronetcy in 1849 for public service, Sir James Kay-Shuttleworth set about making the improvements at Gawthorpe which were to transform his wife's ancestral home. Sadly, chronic ill-health was the scourge of the Kay-Shuttleworths in later life, particularly in respect of Janet, who from 1853 to her death in 1872 stayed almost continuously at health resorts in England, Germany and Italy. Their eldest son, Ughtred, later recalled 'a lamentable estrangement' between Janet and Sir James, caused by 'the distressing ailments of both', combined with 'the almost hypnotic influence' of Janet's inseparable companion, a Prussian governess called Miss Poplawska, who hated Sir James and ruthlessly kept Janet at a distance from him. Nevertheless there was a frequent exchange of letters, and apparently a death-bed reconciliation.

Sir James Kay-Shuttleworth

Dr James Phillips Kay, the son of a Rochdale cotton manufacturer, achieved distinction as a physician in Manchester from 1827 but left the medical profession in 1835. According to a colleague, he had 'engaged in politics more eagerly than was prudent or consistent with medical success'. Instead he turned his energies to social reform, first as an Assistant Poor Law Commissioner and from 1839 as Secretary to the newly-formed Education Committee of the Privy Council. In his ten years in that office he almost single-handedly laid the foundations of a public education system, but his health collapsed in 1848 and he retired the following year with a baronetcy. His marriage to Janet Shuttleworth in 1842 had placed him in charge of the Gawthorpe estate, and in 1849 he commissioned the architect Charles Barry, a personal friend since at least 1840, to undertake a major restoration of the Hall. 'My house improvements will I think make 'old Giggy' wear a new face', he wrote in 1851. 'Barry & I are rather ostentatious folks when we set to work.'

Above Sir James Kay-Shuttleworth, 1st Bt (1804–77). From an early photograph, c.1865

Charlotte Brontë

The novelist Charlotte Brontë visited Gawthorpe in March 1850. The Hall was much to her taste – she described it to a friend as 'grey, antique, castellated and stately' – while the Kay-Shuttleworths were of still more interest to her. She described Janet as having 'frankness, good-humour, and activity', without pretension to aristocratic airs, but seeming to lack the 'grace, dignity, fine feeling' which Sir James possessed. Sir James was 'a man of polished manners, with clear intellect and highly cultivated mind'. He was not frank, 'but, on the contrary, politic', being 'courtly and affable in some points of view', and 'strict and rigorous in others'.

Charlotte rejoined the Kay-Shuttleworths in August 1850 in the Lake District, where they introduced her to Mrs Gaskell, her future biographer. Here she was more inspired by the scenery than the conversations with her host: 'Sometimes, while [Sir James] was warning me against the faults of the artist-class, all the while vagrant artist instincts were busy in the mind of his listener.' However, Sir James meant well, and when Charlotte revisited Gawthorpe in January 1855 with her husband, the Rev. Arthur Bell Nicholls, he offered Nicholls the living of Habergham church. But the offer was declined, and after the couple had returned home, Charlotte fell ill and died.

Above Charlotte Brontë (1816–55); chalk drawing by George Richmond, 1850 (National Portrait Gallery)

The Shuttleworth Family

The 20th century

Ennobled in peace and war

Sir Ughtred Kay-Shuttleworth, 2nd Bt and later 1st Baron Shuttleworth, inherited the Gawthorpe estates on his mother's death in 1872, a year after his marriage to Blanche Parish, daughter of the diplomat Sir Woodbine Parish. He, like his 18th-century forbears, followed a parliamentary career, as Liberal MP for Hastings from 1869 and for Clitheroe from 1885 until his elevation to the peerage (for political services) in 1902. For 20 years from 1908 he was Lord Lieutenant of Lancashire, and in 1913 entertained the King and Queen at Gawthorpe.

Lord Shuttleworth's two sons were both lost during the First World War. The elder son, Lawrence, was killed in action in March 1917, and the younger son, Edward, was killed three months later in a motorcycle accident on military service. Thereafter Lord Shuttleworth retired to Barbon, the family estate in Westmorland, where he lived – virtually blind and bedridden after about 1930 – until his death in 1939 at the age of 95.

By another sad turn of fate, Lord Shuttleworth's two grandsons Richard and Ronald, who became 2nd and 3rd Lord Shuttleworth respectively, were both killed in the Second World War. Richard, elder son of Lawrence, served with Fighter Command in the Battle of Britain and was shot down over the Channel in August 1940. Ronald, the

Above The Hon. Rachel Kay-Shuttleworth (1886–1967); by Peter Brannan, 1960

younger son, was killed on active service in North Africa in 1942. The title then passed to a cousin, Charles, only son of Edward Kay-Shuttleworth; he also suffered in the War, being severely injured in the Western Desert, where he lost a leg and had the other paralysed.

Charles, 4th Lord Shuttleworth returned to Gawthorpe and in 1947 married Anne, daughter of Col. Geoffrey Phillips. Gawthorpe, however, was not a practical residence for a disabled owner, and in 1953, when the house had become surrounded by open-cast coal mining, he moved north to Leck Hall, near Kirkby Lonsdale, leaving Gawthorpe in the care of his aunt, the Hon. Rachel Kay-Shuttleworth.

'Miss Rachel', as she was widely known, was prodigiously active in social welfare work in Lancashire, but that aspect is less well known than her talent as an embroideress, and as a teacher and collector of embroidery. She

Left Sir Ughtred Kay-Shuttleworth, 2nd Bt, later 1st Lord Shuttleworth (1844–1939); by John Collier, 1884

Left Major Charles, 4th Lord Shuttleworth (1917–75); by Derek Hill, 1962

Right Blanche, Lady Kay-Shuttleworth, later 1st Lady Shuttleworth (1851–1924); by John Collier, 1884

envisaged her great collection of textiles as the basis of a 'craft house', where textile crafts might be learnt and practised. Her vision was realised in 1970, when Lord Shuttleworth gave Gawthorpe Hall to the National Trust, with a 99-year lease to Lancashire County Council for public opening and educational use.

When Lord Shuttleworth died in 1975, he was succeeded by his son Charles, 5th Lord Shuttleworth, a chartered surveyor. Living at Leck Hall with his wife Ann, he has generously made available much of the original furniture for display at Gawthorpe, and continues to maintain a lively interest in the home of his ancestors.

Below left Charles, 5th Lord Shuttleworth; by Richard Foster, 1973

Below right Ann, 5th Lady Shuttleworth; by Richard Foster, 1975

The Shuttleworths of Gawthorpe

Owners of Gawthorpe are set in **bold** type

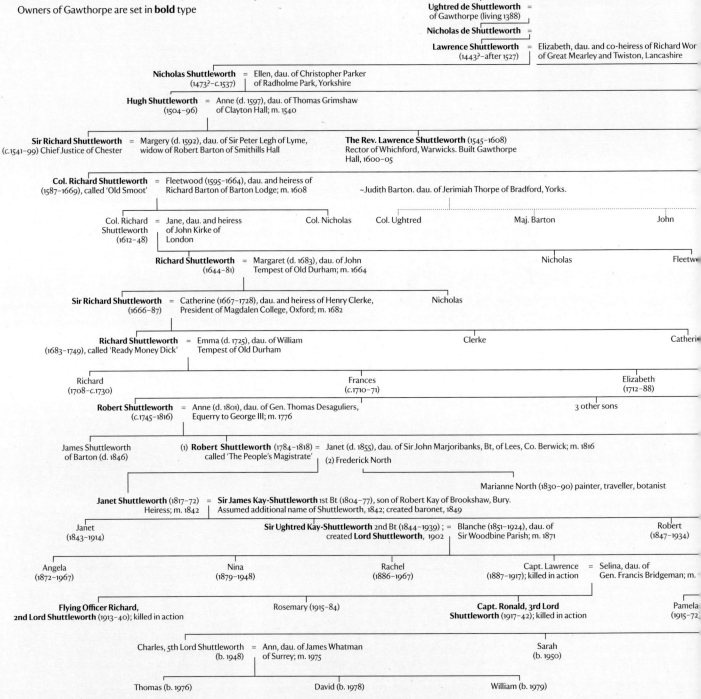

Henry de Shuttleworth of Shuttleworth Hall = Agnes, dau. and heiress of William de Hacking of Hacking Hall

Ughtred de Shuttleworth of Gawthorpe (living 1388) =

Nicholas de Shuttleworth

Lawrence Shuttleworth (1443?–after 1527) = Elizabeth, dau. and co-heiress of Richard Wor of Great Mearley and Twiston, Lancashire

Nicholas Shuttleworth (1473?–c.1537) = Ellen, dau. of Christopher Parker of Radholme Park, Yorkshire

Hugh Shuttleworth (1504–96) = Anne (d. 1597), dau. of Thomas Grimshaw of Clayton Hall; m. 1540

Sir Richard Shuttleworth (c.1541–99) Chief Justice of Chester = Margery (d. 1592), dau. of Sir Peter Legh of Lyme, widow of Robert Barton of Smithills Hall

The Rev. Lawrence Shuttleworth (1545–1608) Rector of Whichford, Warwicks. Built Gawthorpe Hall, 1600–05

Col. Richard Shuttleworth (1587–1669), called 'Old Smoot' = Fleetwood (1595–1664), dau. and heiress of Richard Barton of Barton Lodge; m. 1608

~Judith Barton. dau. of Jerimiah Thorpe of Bradford, Yorks.

Col. Richard Shuttleworth (1612–48) = Jane, dau. and heiress of John Kirke of London

Col. Nicholas

Col. Ughtred

Maj. Barton

John

Richard Shuttleworth (1644–81) = Margaret (d. 1683), dau. of John Tempest of Old Durham; m. 1664

Nicholas

Fleetw

Sir Richard Shuttleworth (1666–87) = Catherine (1667–1728), dau. and heiress of Henry Clerke, President of Magdalen College, Oxford; m. 1682

Nicholas

Richard Shuttleworth (1683–1749), called 'Ready Money Dick' = Emma (d. 1725), dau. of William Tempest of Old Durham

Clerke

Catheri

Richard (1708–c.1730)

Frances (c.1710–71)

Elizabeth (1712–88)

Robert Shuttleworth (c.1745–1816) = Anne (d. 1801), dau. of Gen. Thomas Desaguliers, Equerry to George III; m. 1776

3 other sons

James Shuttleworth of Barton (d. 1846)

(1) **Robert Shuttleworth** (1784–1818) called 'The People's Magistrate' = Janet (d. 1855), dau. of Sir John Marjoribanks, Bt, of Lees, Co. Berwick; m. 1816

(2) Frederick North

Marianne North (1830–90) painter, traveller, botanist

Janet Shuttleworth (1817–72) Heiress; m. 1842 = **Sir James Kay-Shuttleworth** 1st Bt (1804–77), son of Robert Kay of Brookshaw, Bury. Assumed additional name of Shuttleworth, 1842; created baronet, 1849

Janet (1843–1914)

Sir Ughtred Kay-Shuttleworth 2nd Bt (1844–1939) ; created **Lord Shuttleworth**, 1902 = Blanche (1851–1924), dau. of Sir Woodbine Parish; m. 1871

Robert (1847–1934)

Angela (1872–1967)

Nina (1879–1948)

Rachel (1886–1967)

Capt. Lawrence (1887–1917); killed in action = Selina, dau. of Gen. Francis Bridgeman; m.

Flying Officer Richard, 2nd Lord Shuttleworth (1913–40); killed in action

Rosemary (1915–84)

Capt. Ronald, 3rd Lord Shuttleworth (1917–42); killed in action

Pamela (1915–72.

Charles, 5th Lord Shuttleworth (b. 1948) = Ann, dau. of James Whatman of Surrey; m. 1975

Sarah (b. 1950)

Thomas (b. 1976)

David (b. 1978)

William (b. 1979)

Henry   Ellen   Elizabeth

Bernard   Richard   Elizabeth

Thomas Shuttleworth   =   Anne (*c.*1569–1637)   2 daughters
(1546–93)   dau. of Richard Lever
             of Little Lever, Lancashire; m.1586

Nicholas   Ughtred   3 daughters

Edward   Captain William;   Thomas   3 daughters
             killed in action, 1643

James Shuttleworth   =   Mary (1718–91), dau. and heiress of Robert Holden   2 other sons
(1714–73)   of Aston Hall, Derbyshire; m. 1742
             2 daughters

Richard   6 daughters

Lionel   Stuart
(1849–1900)   (1851–87)

Capt. Edward   =   Sibell, dau. of   Catherine
(1890–1917); killed in a motorcycle   Charles Adeane of Brabraham Hall,   (1894–1963)
accident on military service   Cambridge; m. 1914

Major Charles, 4th Lord Shuttleworth (1917–75)   =   Anne (d. 1991), dau. of Col. Geoffrey
Gave Gawthorpe Hall to the National Trust, 1970   Phillips; m. 1947

Robert   Edward
(b. 1954)   (b. 1962)

Overleaf **Minton floor tiles
in the Porch**

Manuscript sources

Most of the Shuttleworth family papers relating to Gawthorpe are deposited in the Lancashire Record Office, Preston. They date from the 14th century onwards and include the Rev. Lawrence Shuttleworth's building accounts for the Hall, contained in four of the nine surviving household and estate account books of 1582–1621. A selection from the accounts was published by the Chetham Society in the 1850s. The correspondence of Sir James Kay-Shuttleworth and his family in the 19th century can be found in the John Rylands Library, Manchester; and a further 250 letters of F.H. Groves, the Clerk of Works in 1850-2, are preserved at the Lancashire Record Office with the plans and working drawings of the Barry restoration.

Printed sources

Anon., 'Gawthorpe Hall, Lancashire', *Country Life,* 10 May 1913.

Barry, The Rev. Alfred, *The Life and Works of Sir Charles Barry,* London, 1867.

Bostwick, David, 'The Jacobean plasterwork at Gawthorpe Hall and its sources', *Apollo,* May 1994, pp.24–28.

Conroy, Michael P., *Backcloth to Gawthorpe,* Nelson, 1971, revised 1996.

Conroy, Michael P., *Mysteries and Memorabilia* of *Gawthorpe and the Shuttleworths,* Settle, 2003.

Gaskell, Elizabeth, *The Life of Charlotte Brontë,* London, 1857.

George, David, 'Jacobean Actors and the Great Hall at Gawthorpe, Lancashire', *Theatre Notebook,* Vol. xxxvii, No. 3, 1983, pp.109-20.

Girouard, Mark, *Robert Smythson and the Elizabethan Country House,* Yale University Press, 1983.

Harland, John (ed.), *The House and Farm Accounts of the Shuttleworths of Gawthorpe,* 1582–1621, 4 parts, Chetham Society, 1856-8.

Jervis, Simon, 'Gawthorpe Revived', *Country Life,* 11 June 1987, pp.96-101.

Parry, Linda, 'Gathering Inspiration', *Country Life,* 9 June 1988, pp.248-9.

Robinson, John Martin, 'Gawthorpe Hall, Lancashire', *Country Life,* 4 and 11 September 1973, pp.558-61, 630-3.

Selleck, R.J.W., *James Kay-Shuttleworth: Journey of an Outsider,* Ilford, 1994.

Shorter, Clement, *The Brontës and their Circle,* London, 1914.

Smith, Frank, *The Life and Work of Sir James Kay-Shuttleworth,* London, 1923.

Victoria County History, Lancashire, London, 1911, Vol. 6, pp.463-7.

Whitaker, The Rev. Thomas Dunham, *History of the Original Parish of Whalley,* 2nd edn., 1806, 3rd edn., London, 1818.

Williams, Canon G. A., *Rachel Kay-Shuttleworth,* Kendal, 1968.

Electronic sources

Descriptions and images of objects on display in the furnished rooms at Gawthorpe Hall can be found on the National Trust's collections website, **www.nationaltrustcollections.org.uk** For further information about the Gawthorpe Textiles Collection, visit **www.gawthorpetextiles.org.uk**